Other Books by MikWright

hey, girl!

happy birthday . . .
blah, blah, blah

who's your daddy?

your mother looks good . . .

MikWright . . . family style

mixed nuts

drinks well with others

momma loves her some eggnog

don't blame me

sister

i told you not to use
it in the bathtub

MikWright

**Andrews McMeel
Publishing, LLC**

Kansas City

07 08 09 10 11 TWP 10 9 8 7 6 5 4 3 2

ISBN-13: 978-0-7407-6878-1
ISBN-10: 0-7407-6878-6

Library of Congress Control Number:
2007924478

www.andrewsmcmeel.com
www.mikwright.com

Authors' photos by Jason Kinney

ATTENTION: SCHOOLS AND BUSINESSES
Andrews McMeel books are available at quantity
discounts with bulk purchase for educational,
business, or sales promotional use. For
information, please write to: Special Sales
Department, Andrews McMeel Publishing, LLC,
4520 Main Street, Kansas City, Missouri 64111.

We would like to dedicate
don't blame me, sister
to Sister Mary McCluney. As a friend
and steward to many, Sister Mary
exudes a spirit that has and will
change the world forever.
We love you!

Tim and Phyllis

When the hair pulling is done and you've held her down and snapped her bra, simmer down. She is your sister and she did get you that hot date with the fragile four-eyed football statistician.

In *don't blame me, sister* MikWright zeros in on sisters, mothers, crazy aunts, and more. But, at the end of the day, a sister is your phone-a-friend, your quick-fix hug, and your best friend.

Rock on, sister!

who can turn the world on
with her smile?

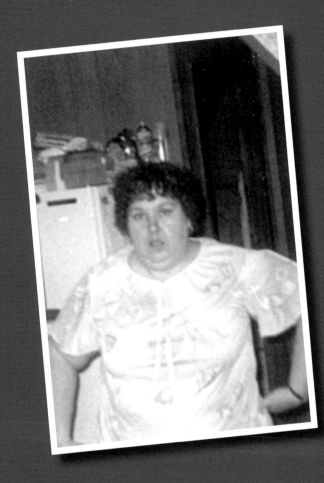

maureen, he's everything i've

ever wanted in a man . . .

tall, dark, and on top of me.

the world doesn't
revolve around you . . .
you're just dizzy.

if a bear shits in the woods,
should i have a cocktail?

it's all about the shoes.

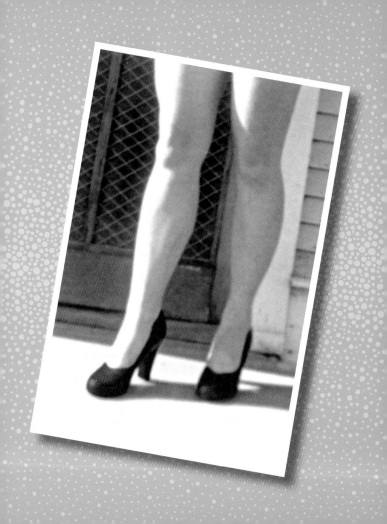

do i look like a people person?

the secret to a long,
healthy, happy life is a
good bowel movement.

jeanie had her ultrasound today and the doctor believes it's a girl (or a boy with a very small penis).

ma'am, the good news is
your furnace can be fixed
by monday. the bad news is
your makeup is all wrong.

don't blame me, wanda!
i specifically told you it
took four "d" size batteries and
not to use it in the bathtub.

are you out of your mind
sleeping with someone you
don't know? save that for
when you're married.

don't hate me because
i'm fabulous.

the results of your
color analysis are in.
you look good in nothing.

you know, with everybody
getting laid off, i'm just
wondering when i'm going
to get laid on.

click here to enlarge.

if you can't say something
nice about someone,
i want to hear it.

next time would
it be too much to
ask for a hard-bodied,
tight-assed stripper?

oh, lookie here . . .
cora passed. i knew i'd
outlive that tramp.

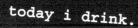

today i drink.

yesterday i drank.

tomorrow i'll be drunk.

i was never meant to work.

listen here, you flat-chested, broad-assed, penciled-in eyebrowed, tupperware-snatchin' wench! give me back my deviled egg carrier.

for the life of me, i don't know
how i got that yeast infection.
i was in and out of that bakery
in less than a minute.

we ended the relationship
as friends. you can
e-mail him at
lying-cheating-son-of-a-bitch.com.

i was never meant
to fly coach!

hmmm.

it eats.

it sleeps.

it poops.

it already takes after dad.

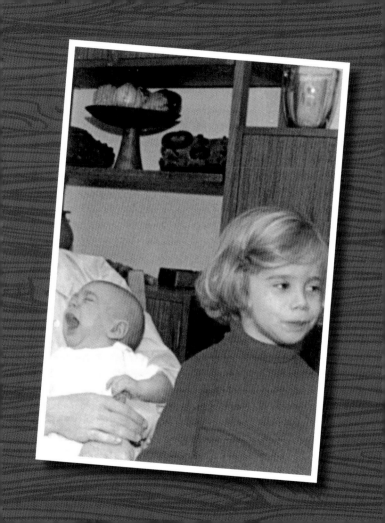

sleeps well with others.

when it comes to dieting,
remember one simple rule . . .
"if you can't lose it,
decorate it."

i'm not here to make things
better, only to observe and
pass judgment.

girl, you keep talkin'
but you ain't sayin' nothin'.

jane likes dick.
dick has a big . . .

                    rooster.

she ain't heavy.
she's my sister.

sometimes you just gotta
turn the other cheek.

honey, you didn't hear
it from me, but she can get
her legs so far in the air it
takes an air traffic controller
to bring 'em down.

if there is a god, please
let this guy be my ob-gyn.

don't look so sad, eunice.
it makes me equally upset to
have someone call me sir.

hence the age-old question:

which came first . . .

the polyester or the peroxide?